The Grand Grimore

The Grand Grimore or Imperial Ritual of Magic
Compiled by: Pythagoras 38 (Reuben Swinburne Clymer)

Cover image: *Dixit Eloim eres cite multiple animal in terra*
(God said, Let the earth bring forth living creatures)
Lay-out: www.burokd.nl

ISBN 978-94-92355-66-9

VAMzzz Publishing
P.O. Box 3340
1001 AC Amsterdam
The Netherlands
www.vamzzz.com
vamzzz@protonmail.com

THE GRAND GRIMORE
OR IMPERIAL RITUAL OF MAGIC

Compiled by
Pythagoras 38

Pythagoras 38, Supreme Master of the Order (Reuben Swinburne Clymer)
November 25, 1878 - June 3, 1966

contents

Including Full Instructions in Making of the Magic Rod, Talismans, Amulets and Rings. Private Instructions in Crystal and Magic Mirror Initiation, in Magran Magic and Spiritualism.

Compiled by Pythagoras, 38
Supreme Master of the Temple

NOTICE

This whole work is in the "Code" of the Order, and no one must attempt to follow any of the instructions, or even believe in the writings unless they have the "Key" thereto.

To All Students

You must strictly observe the following regulations.

To make it impossible for our writings, books, letters, etc., ever falling into wrong hands, not even in case of the sudden decease of a member, all are solemnly obligated to the following:

All printed matter, letters, etc., in short, all things relating to the Imperialistic Order are to be kept in a locked portfolio or casket, which must bear the inscription:

"Property of the Imperialistic Council and Venerable Order of Magi.
"To be forwarded to The Philosophical Publishing Co., Dept. B, Allentown, Pa.

"1st. Should I be taken suddenly ill.
2nd. Go upon a long journey whereby I may be cut off from communicating with them.
3rd. In case of my death or serions accident.

"This portfolio or its contents must be at once forwarded to the above address, who, in case of 1st or 2nd, will return the same as soon as the obstacles are removed, and, in case of death, will demand this portfolio or casket as the property of the Order.

"PYTHAGORAS, 38."

FOREWORD

In placing this second and highest work of the Order into your hands it is necessary to say but a few words regarding it.

Some students have an idea that there is something new in Magic. There is not, for the more we study the old Masters the more we find out how absolutely ignorant we are concerning the hidden forces known to them.

There is but one thing which we of the present age can give to the beginner, and that is the Key to the old writings, for these are in such language as to mislead practically all but the greatest of teachers.

The "Grand Grimore," often called "Book of Black Magic," because absolutely misunderstood, contains practically all that is known concerning Magic. This same remark may be made concerning "The Key of Solomon the King," but, right here, we must bear in mind that the "Grand Grimore" is simply the "Key of Solomon the King" in the Gothic form. Thus the two are identical but used by a different people.

In this present work we wish to give credit to whom credit is due, and as the authority of the Imperialistic Council is founded upon that of the old Masters we wish it understood that we are simply following the old Masters, giving you their knowledge, but in a modern and practical form.

Concerning certain books issued by so-called Masters, we wish to be distinctly understood that these are issued without authority, and, what is more, without credit being given to the original authors, which is the worst feature.

To the proofs: –

We turn to page 44 of this so-called great work and we find the instructions concerning Alchemy, word for word, as that given by Barrett in his "Book of the Magi," page 44. Not a word of credit is given, and the instructions are in the original form without any explanation.

We turn to page 39 of the same work and we find that it is Barrett's, word for word on same page of the "Book of the Magi."

In fact, this so-called great work is practically chapter for chapter that of the "Book of the Magi" by Barrett. It contains the cuts, images, etc., of Barrett, and even the "Eiographia Antigua."

There is no harm in republishing old books, but it is a serious thing for a man to call himself a High Caste Adept and Magician, boldly steal the work of the old Masters and without giving a word of credit. It is this which is serious and damnable.

Do not think that we say this without absolute proof in the form of books by the old Masters themselves, and these are open for inspection by any Officer of the Law or by the student.

It is needless to say who this publisher is, for the publishers of the Magazine "The Kalpaka," known as the "Latent Light Culture," Tinnevelly Bridge, South India, have exposed his method pretty thoroughly for stealing the private lessons known as "India's Hood Unveiled; Occult Mysteries Revealed," and publishing them in book form without giving credit and without authority.

I regret that it is necessary to say this much, but as it is our duty to warn our Brothers against the false, we must do this.

Besides this, all the instructions of the old Masters are given in crude form, which was intended to deceive and consequently the modern reader of these works is deceived.

Concerning the two private chapters on the Crystal and the Magic Mirror and Spiritual Development, we wish it to be distinctly understood that these are according to the teachings of Dr. P. B. Randolph, without the slightest doubt the greatest Master of any age. It was Dr. Randolph that brought these Mysteries to America. It was he who first taught the mysteries of the Soul, of Immortality, of Mysticism, of the Magic Mirror, Clairvoyance, etc., to the people of America, and all the present works on the subject are saturated with his teachings, but not one, without any exception, has given him a line of credit. If you have any doubts concerning what is said here, you will only need to obtain his works, and the proofs will be before you.

Regarding Magean Magic, we need only say that they are the best instructions to be had. There can be NONE more simple or more powerful than these. It is the Old Magean Magic with the crude ceremonial part eliminated. It is the kernel of the nut. The meat without the shell.

If you follow the spirit of these instructions faithfully then you must succeed. Failure is then impossible.

Concerning the Talismans, we need say that we herein give you the most secret instructions of the Order, in that we show you how to make these under the signs of the Planets which rule them, instead of under the crude, laborious, ceremonial form.

Praying that you may ever remain faithful to the Sublime Order,

Fraternally yours,
PYTHAGORAS, 38,
Supreme Master of the Order.

THE ART OF INVOKING SPIRITS IN THE CRYSTAL

Containing full instructions concerning the work, both ancient and modern.

ANCIENT – THE "GRAND GRIMORE"

The Art of Invoking Spirits in the Crystal, or the process of Spiritual Development, has always been a most important part of Divination, and the old "Grand Grimore" states that it was known and practice by the ancients, as all those who read sacred or profane history may discover for themselves. It is further said that the sacred texts contain many references to invocation performed by the Crystal, and, that in the opinion of many learned and eminent men, the *Urim* and *Thummin* of Holy Scripture were used for a similar purpose to that of the lucid pebble in our own day.

The following Ritual is found in the document known as the "Grand Grimore"; it exhibits the methods by which magic in the past produced results that were identical with many which are now obtained in a much simpler manner, with possibly greater success, but which require a longer time and possibly more personal will power. Those who are inclined to attempt the ceremonial experiment may rest assured that the use of an ordinary crystal with the most simple method of mounting will serve the purpose. The proper mode of inscription should be, however, observed, and also the other conditions before and during procedure, as carelessness in this respect is not only calculated to void the experience, but it is dangerous.

All those who wish to obtain the assistance of the Good

Spirits in the Crystal must lead a pure life, keeping themselves, as it were, apart from the things that are vulgar. The invocant must maintain himself in an orderly, clean and pure manner, using frequent ablutions (bathing in cold water being best) and prayers, for at least three days before beginning the work; and the moon should be on the increase. The invocant may, if he wish, have several interested people, as companions, to assist him in the work; but they must all conform to the rules and forms necessary; to be observed in the practice of the great art. He must be firm, daring, strong in faith, filled with great confidence and must be careful that no part of the ceremonies be omitted, if he wish for success in the work. The accomplishment of his design will depend upon the performance of all that is prescribed herein. The invocant may proceed to the work at any time of the year, providing that the two Luminaries, namely, the Sun and Moon, are in a fortunate aspect, with favoring planets; but when the Sun is in his greatest northern declination is the best time.

CONCERNING THE ROOM

In order to carry on his work, the invocant must have a small room in some retired part of the house. It should be devoid of all adornments, since these might distract his attention; but the floor must be perfectly clean, so as to receive the lines of the circle and the characters to be traced thereon. The circle may then be drawn seven feet in diameter and the characters with the holy names inscribed duly and clearly, in accordance with the following model (see Cut A), using charcoal.

The room must be kept free from the hurry of business, as well as from prying and curious intruders, and should be locked when not in use. The invocant must bear in mind that preparation belonging to the art must ever be made during the moon's increase.

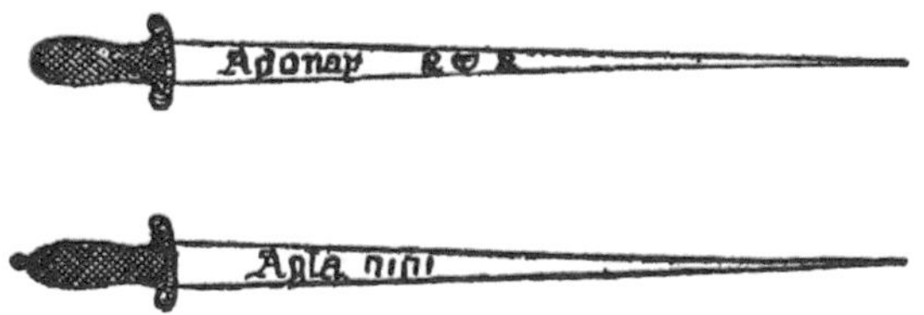

Cut A.

THE APPARATUS AND INSTRUMENTS TO BE USED

The operator must be provided with a small table, covered with a white linen cloth, with a chain, with the necessary materials for a fire, in order to burn the incense proper to the planet governing the hour in which the work is performed; with a torch and two wax candles, placed in brass candlesticks, and engraved, as shown in Cut B, on the pedestals. He must also have a pair of compasses, a knife, a cord, a pair of scissors, a magic sword of pure steel, as shown in Cut A, a magic wand, pens, ink, paper and parchment. All these instruments should be used by him for the first time, but may be used by him always thereafter.

THE CRYSTAL

The invocant must be provided with a crystal; it must be properly polished. In fact, such a one as usually used by the seer. It should be inclosed in some box, made of oak or any other polished material.

The holy names must be written round about it in gold ink. If the oak box is used always, the letters may be written thereon, but in such case it must never be taken from the box. Any suitable will do whereon to place the crystal and the names written.

CONSECRATION OF THE FLOOR

Bless, O Lord, I beseech thee, this ground, even this place, and expel all evil and wickedness from this circle. Sanctify it and make it meet, becoming and convenient for Thy servant to begin and bring to pass therein all his desires, through our Lord and Saviour. Amen.

Be thou blessed, O creature of this crystal, he thou purified and consecrated; in the name of the Father and of the Son and of the Holy Ghost.

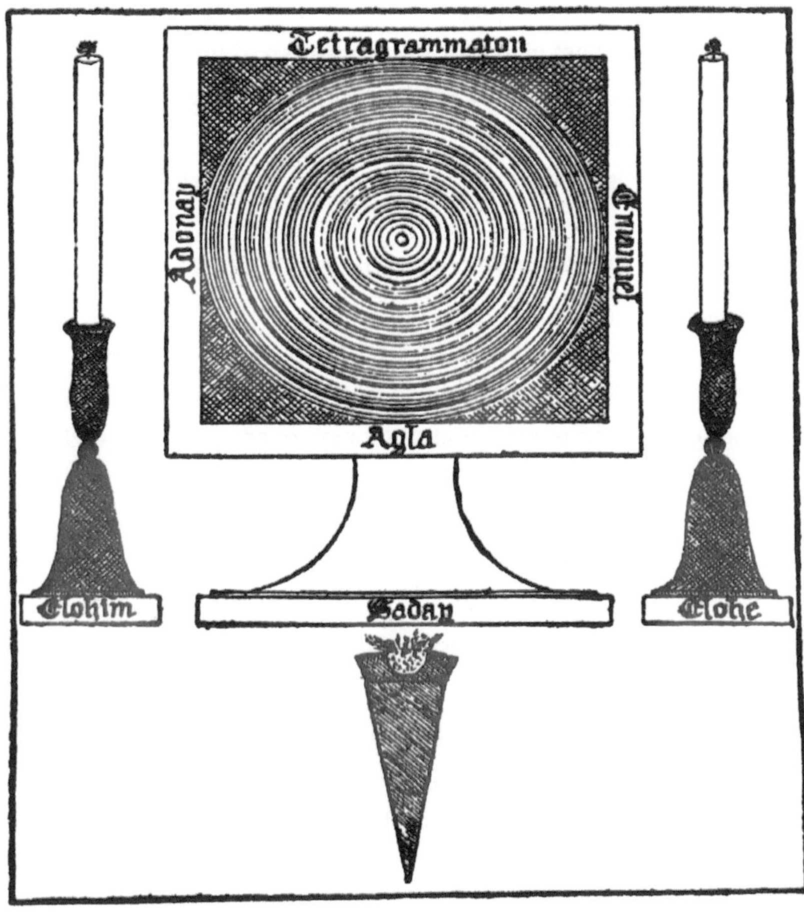

Cut B.

BLESSING THE LIGHTS

In the name of the Father and of the Son and of the Holy Ghost. O, Lord God, the heaven and the earth are full of thy glory, before whose face there is a bright and shining light for ever. Bless now, O Lord, these creatures of light for ever. Bless these creatures of light which Thou hast given for the kindly use of man, that, being sanctified by Thee, they may not be extinguished by the evil power or filthy darkness of evil, but may shine forth brightly and lend their assistance to this holy work, through Christ our Lord. Amen.

CONSECRATION OF THE INSTRUMENTS

O, God Almighty, Thou Who art a God of strength and greatly to be honored. Bless, O Lord, these instruments, that they may be a terror unto the enemy, and that I may overcome therewith all phantasms and oppositions from the evil forces, through Thy influence and the help of Thy holy and mighty names – On, El, Agla, *Tetragrammation* – and in the Cross of Christ, our Lord. Amen.

CONSECRATION OF THE CRYSTAL

O *Eternal* God, Who by Thy wisdom hast appointed great power to the characters and other holy writings of Thy spirits and hast given unto them that use them faithfully the power to work many things thereby: Bless this crystal, O Lord, formed, framed and written by the hand of Thy servant; that being filled with divine virtue and influence by Thy command, O most holy God, it may show forth its power and virtue, to Thy praise and glory, through Christ, our Lord and Saviour. Amen.

I bless and consecrate this crystal, in the name of the Father and the Son and the Holy Ghost.

In consecrating all the instruments and other things necessary in this art, the invocant must repeat the forms of consecration while placing his hand upon the different articles, having his face turned towards the East. These preliminaries being finished, he may place the table in front of the circle, with the crystal thereon, the two candlesticks – one of them on either side – the remaining apparatus ready at hand. He may then enter the circle – with his companions – if any – on the day and hour of Mercury – the moon increasing – and begin the operations by invoking – with all the power of his being – the Spirit *Vassago*.

THE INVOCATION

I exorcise, call upon and command the Spirit Vassago, by and in the name of the Immense and Everlasting God, Jehovah, Adonai, Elohim, Agla, On, Tetragrammation, and by and in the name of our Lord and Saviour Jesus Christ, the only Son of the Eternal and True God, Creator of heaven and earth and all that is therein – Filius, Sother, Emanuel, Primogenitus, Homousien, Benus, Via, Veritas, Sapientia, Virtus, Lex, Paster, Propheta, Sacredos, Athanatos, Paracletus, Alpha and Omega – by all these high, great, glorious, royal and ineffable names of the omnipotent God and of His only Son, our Lord and Saviour Jesus Christ, the Second Essence of the Glorious Trinity: I exercise, command, call upon and conjure thee – Spirit Vassago – wheresoever thou art, East, West, North or South, or being bound to any one under the compass of the heavens, that thou mayst come immediately from the place of thy private abode and appear to me visibly in fair and decent form within this crystal, stone or glass. I do again exercise and command thee powerfully – Spirit Vassago to come and appear visibly before me in this crystal, stone or glass, in a fair, solid and decent form. And yet again I do bind strongly and command thee – Spirit Vassago – to appear and help me to obtain – (mention the desire) – even by the virtue and power of those names whereby I can bind all rebellious, obstinate, refractory spirits – Alla, Carital, Maribal, Carion, Urien, Spyton, Lorean, Marmos, Agaion, Cados, Yron, Astron, Gardeong, Tetragrammation, Strallax, Spignos, Sother, Jah, On, El, Elohim – by all aforesaid – I command thee – Spirit Vassago – to make haste, come away and do my bidding, as aforesaid, without further tarrying: In the name of Him Who shall come to judge the quick and the dead, and the world of fire. Amen.

The invocant will gaze into the heart of the crystal while giving this command. After it is given he or she should continue to gaze into the crystal for from ten to fifteen minutes and hold the thought of what is desired.

Do not expect the spirit to appear visibly before you, for this seldom happens, although your desire may become personified in visible form in the crystal.

After gazing the required length of time, it is necessary to release the spirit in the following manner:

LICENSE TO DEPART

Forasmuch as thou camest in peace and quietness, and hast answered unto my petition, I give humble and sincere thanks unto Almighty God, in Whose name I called thee, in Whose name also thou camest; and now mayst then depart in peace, to me again returning, at what time soever I shall call thee by thine oath, or by thy name, by thine order or thine office, which is granted from the Creator. And the power of God be with me and thee, and upon the whole issue of God. Amen.

The invocant should follow this drill every evening until the desired object has been accomplished. In this form of development the Neophyte must not start until he knows that he can continue regularly until his desire has been accomplished.

THE MODERN INITIATION OF THE CRYSTAL

MODERN – ROSICRUCIAN SYSTEM

Clairvoyance is the art and power of knowing or cognizing facts, things and principles by methods totally distinct from those usually pursued in their attainment.

We are approaching the termination of the present civilization, are bidding farewell to many of its modes, moods, opinions, sentiments, thoughts and procedures, and are entering upon a new epoch of human history and might, destined to *develop* powers in man, now latent mainly, but which are destined to revolutionize the globe. On earth man is greatest, mind the greatest part of man, and clairvoyance the greatest part of mind.

Clairvoyance depends upon a peculiar condition of the nerves and brain. The present instructions consist in the knowledge of the exact method *how*, the precise time *where*, and the proper time *when*.

At first, clairvoyance, like any movement, nervous or muscular, requires a special effort, but it soon becomes automatic, involuntary, mechanical. Keep your design constantly before you, and your soul and inner senses will make grooves for themselves, and continue to move in them as cars on rails or wheels in ruts. Let your groove be clairvoyance.

Lucidity is no gift, but a universal possibility common to the human race. It is latent, or *still* mind-power, and can be brought to the surface in a majority of cases. *Omnia vincit labor!*

All mental action comes through nervous action, but in these cases the results must be reached outside our usual mental habitudes and paths. The person who attempts to reach clairvoyance and gets discouraged after a few trials does not deserve the power. If you begin, *keep right on.* Every experiment lands you one step nearer success, and that, too, whether you aim at Psychometry, Lucidity, or any of the fifty phases or grades.

Remember that physical conditions influence, modify and determine mental states, whether these be normal or recondite and mysterious.

Nor forget that pure blood gives pure power. If your blood is foul, do not attempt clairvoyance till you are free from it. Artists prepare their paints, you must prepare your body; else no good picture comes, no lucidity follows. Sound lungs, stomach, kidneys, liver, brain, blood, heart and pelvic apparatus are necessary. Above all, the blood must be purified, vacated of its poisens, rheums, etc., and be tuned up to the concert pitch, if you would enjoy the music of the spheres, and know beyond your outer knowing.

Food, digestion, drink, sleep, must be attended to. True clairvoyance is coincident only with normal appetites normally sated. Excess destroys it. Every passion, except the grosser, has a normal sphere.

Clairvoyance is qualitative and quantitative, like all other mental forces. It is limited, fragmentary, incomplete, in all, because we are all imperfect, *but* no other being can occupy your ground, or be so great in your respective direction. No one exactly like you; and you precisely like nobody else. We are like the world – green spots and deserts; arid here, frozen there; fertile in one spot, sterile in another; therefore we should cultivate our *special loves.* Clairvoyant vigor demands attention to the law. The eternal equation of vital vigor is – rest equals exercise. Remember this and retain your power.

Clairvoyance is an affair of the air, food, drink, love, passion, light, sleep, health, rest, sunshine, joy, music, laber, exercise, lungs, liver, blood, quite as much as of magnetic coma, for all mental operations are physically conditioned.

Clairvoyance is an art like any other. The elements exist, but to be useful must be systematized. It has hitherto been pursued, not rationally, but empirically; as a blind habit, a sort of gymnastic, a means to delude people, and scarce ever under intelligent guidance like the logical or mathematical or musical faculties of the soul, albeit more valuable than either, and like them, too, subject to the laws of growth. It is far-reaching, and once attained, though the road is difficult, amply repays the time and labor spent.

The mystic ground has hitherto been the prolific hotbed of a host of noxious, dangerous superstitions and quackeries; and this is the first attempt to reclaim it to rational investigation. Clairvoyance is a generic name employed to express various degrees and modes of perception, whereby one is enabled to cognize and know facts, things and principles; or to contact certain knowledge, without the use, and independent of, the ordinary avenues of sense. It is produced or attained in various degrees, by different methods, and is of widely diverse grades and kinds.

In our ordinary state, we see through a glass, darkly; in clairvoyance, we see with more or less distinctness; in intuition, the highest quality of the human mind, we *leap* to results at a single bound and this can come to many through soul development. There are hundreds who imagine they possess one or all of them faculties or qualifications, and arrogate much importance, merely because the ideas have made such a strong impression on their minds; or perhaps they have seen one or two visions or spectral sparks or flashes. Such are what they claim to be, only in the wish. They need training. For clairvoyance is a thing or actual system, rule and law, and whoever would have it in its completeness or *completely*, must conform to the science thereof.

Clairvoyance, or actual *perception*, is of various kinds and degrees. It does not require brilliant talents for its development, for many seers are inferior organically, cerebrally and intellectually, yet the higher and nobler, more brilliant, and finely constituted, the person is, the higher and nobler the clairvoyance they will develop. Some subjects can never get beyond the power to reach the scientific plane, while but a few attain that magnificent sweep of intellect and vision that leaps the world's barriers, forces the gates of death, and revels in the sublime mysteries of the universe. The purer the subject, the better the faculty. Goodness, not mere knowledge, is power. Remember this.

No two persons' clairvoyance are precisely alike. Each clairvoyant has a personal idiosyncrasy that invariably determines his or her specialty, and, whatever that specialty may be, should be encouraged, for in that he or she will excel, and in no other. The attempt to force nature will be so much lost time and wasted effort. *Adopt a specialty and stick to it.*

When any effort towards lucidity bids fair, by care, patience and perseverance, to become a success, and the subject becomes dreamy, or else sees flashes, sparks, white clouds, rolling balls of light vapor, or is partially lucid, the tendency of the mind should be carefully noted, and the future direction of the power or faculty be fully decided on, sought for, aimed at, and strictly, persistently, faithfully followed, until a splendid, and never-to-be-doubted triumph and success crowns the effort.

Decide upon one thing or one plane that you wish to attain and then stick to that until you meet with complete success.

There are various kinds, as well as degrees, of clairvoyance. Natural, intellectual, spiritual and divine, social, practical and purely mental. Or a clear seeing of material forms; lucidity of mind generally; lucidity of special cerebral organs; lucidity upon certain points, as Medicine, Spiritualism, Religion, Philosophy, Science, Logic, Art, Love, etc.

Special cerebral organs become lucid, soon succeeded by an entire illumination of the brain. This is a grand, a sublime, a holy degree, for the subject sees, senses, feels, knows, by a royal power, in on rapport with a thousand knowledges. A step further, a step inward, and the subject is in harmony with both the upper and lower universe. It is when he reaches this state that he is the perfect occult or magical master. He or she is thenceforth a power in the world. All clairvoyance may not claim genius, but all true genius is clairvoyant. Mere talents are dry leaves, tossed up and down by gusts of passion, and scattered and swept away; but genius lies on the bosom of memory and gratitude at her feet.

Magnetic or *true* clairvoyance is best brought about by steadily gazing in the depths of a magic mirror or crystal. It is only necessary that the Neophyte have a certain time each evening when he or she can retire into some private room, gaze into the depth of a magic mirror or crystal for fifteen minutes, holding in mind what is specially desired, and the result will be clairvoyance in due time.

All clairvoyants should, to be useful, successful and enduring, cultivate the habit of deep breathing, for all brain power depends upon the lung power, nor can continued ability exist if this be neglected. All clairvoyants should eat the best and purest things attainable. They need not be costly but natural and fresh.

All clairvoyants must use great caution in matters of intoxicants. Abstinence is good, for error in that direction is fatal to clear vision, or its perpetuity when possessed.

All magnetic, odyllic processes are far oftener productive of grand results if conducted in a darkened chamber, than in a light room or one lighted by the sun. Moonlight is best, candlelight is good.

If, at the end of a few experiments, sparks, flashes, streaks of quick and lingering light are seen, then one or two things are probable. First, that the party by continuance and repetition, can be clairvoyant; or, second, if not too scary, these clouds and sparks may resolve themselves into spiritual forms of friends long gone or of spiritual entities.

Persons ambitions to become clairvoyant must not forget that a full habit, amorous pleasures, high living and mental excitement all are disqualifications. The entire diet should be changed; the linens often; the skin, especially the head and hair, scrupulously so; and, to insure success, the food should be very light; fruits, tea and milk may be used freely; but no chocolate, fat, oysters, pastry, and not much sugar. Nor should the person fail to think, wish and *will* the end aimed at continually. This is White Magic.

All magic mirrors and true crystals are based upon the eternal fact, that whatever exists is something; that *thoughts are things*; that spirit is real substance; that all things photograph themselves upon other surfaces; that sensitives can see and contact these shadows, lights, impressions and images, as abundantly demonstrated by Baron von Reichenbach in his researches into the arcana of chemism, light, force and magnetism; also by thousands of others in all lands, and especially in these days, wherein disembodied people project an image of themselves upon paper, the artist sketching the outline with a pencil, thus photographing the supposed dead, recognizable by all who ever saw them when walking in flesh and blood.

It is well established, however some may sneer, that for ages men of the loftiest mental power have used various physical agents as a means of vision, either to bring themselves in contact with the supernal realms of the Aether, or to afford a sensitive surface upon which the attendant dead could, can and do temporarily photograph whatever they choose to. Nor is this all. I know that by a mysterious process, whose principle it is needless here to expound, a mirror or crystal is the best means to accomplish the end in view.

The true clairvoyant in the sublime degree moves and acts above and beyond the tempestuous realms of the passions – defies their utmost power. Passion dulls the soul's best vision. To reach the lofty eminence, the subject's body *must* be purified, and proper preparation made. Food, raiment, hahits must be modified. It is God's highest gift to man, and cannot be had without a struggle.

THE MEANS OF DEVELOPING CONSCIOUS MEDIUMSHIP

PLANCHETTE

Place the beard upon the laps of two persons, lady and gentleman preferred, with the small table upon the board. Place the fingers lightly but firmly, without pressure, upon the table, so as to allow it to move easily and freely. Within one to five minutes the table will commence to move, at first slowly, then faster, and will then be able to talk or answer questions, which it will do rapidly by touching the printed words, or the letters necessary to form words and sentences, with the foreleg or points.

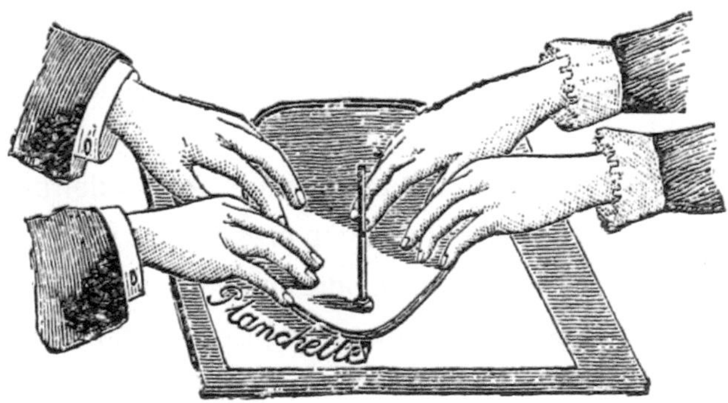

2nd. Care should be taken that one person only should ask questions at a time, so as to avoid confusion, and the questions should be put plainly and accurately.

3rd. To obtain the best results it is important that the persons present should concentrate their minds upon the matter in question and avoid other topics. Have no one at the table who will not sit seriously and respectfully. If you use it in a frivolous spirit, asking ridiculous questions, laughing over it, you naturally get undeveloped influences around you.

4th. The Planchette Indicator is a great mystery, and it is impossible to give exact directions for its management, at all times, and under all circumstances, but with reasonable patience and judgment, it will mere than satisfy the greatest expectations.

5th. In putting the table together wet the tops of the legs and drive them firmly into the table; care should be taken that they are firm and tight.

6th. The board should be kept smooth and free from dust and moisture, as all depends upon the ease with which the feet of the table can glide over the surface of the board. Rubbing with a dry silk handkerchief just before using is advised.

RULES FOR DEVELOPING MEDIUMSHIP

It is certain that the dead cannot appear except under peculiar conditions, as to time, locality and in presence of particular chemical, magnetical, electrical, odic and mechanical states; thus, certain houses, haunted by them, cease to be troubled after being opened, aired, ventilated or partially torn down. It thus becomes clear that some peculiar element, gas, fluid, ether, magnetic, odic, or electrical is absolutely necessary in order that the dead may be able to prove in a physical manner the grand fact of the soul's existence after death.

It is equally certain that the identical elements, whatever they may be, which afford the dead the means of manifestation, are the very ones essential to successful magnetization, and the development of clear somnambulic sight or psycho-vision, for both spiritual-materialization and clairvoyance flourish best coincident with each other; and both unquestionably depend upon the existence of an impalpable, but positive *aura* sphere or air, existent in space generally, evolved by nearly all bodies and forms of matter in limited quantities in condensed form, but occasionally given forth in large volume from the bodies of peculiarly constituted persons, who then are known under the generic titles of clairvoyants, extatics and mediums.

There are two general classes of human organizations – the blonde, or light, who are electric; and the dark, who are almost wholly magnetic. Both these classes are mediumistic; but the dark are very seldom capable of evolving the peculiar sphere or aura, which is essential to the production of phenomena purely physical in its characteristics. But occasionally a brunette from some peculiarity does become a medium for material demonstrations, and when they are so, they excel. But as a general rule the dark person becomes what is known as a speaking medium, or spiritproxy, else become inspirational orators and exalted proclaimers of new, and in some respects, startling, radical and iconoclastic thought, not reducible to any system.

The light persons, generally females, become either physical media of either the positive or negative sort, else they launch out into independent clairvoyance. Mediumship of either kind can easily be reached.

If two wish to develop by the use of the Planchette, it is best that it should be a dark and a light person and, if possible, a man and a woman. One alone can develop just as well as two, but more time is required for the transfusion of the personal aura into the Planchette.

The person who seeks development must persevere, for to begin and then stop is to lose time. There are usually two motives inspiring seekers after mediumship, viz: Love and Money. One seeks it as a means of living; the other to know, to love, to reach the inner and nobler life. One class is nearly soulless, the other, all soul. The entire social, conjural and domestic worlds to-day are in an uproar, chaos and revolution. Were it not so, spiritual intercourse on a large scale were impossible.

There is a morbid and healthy mediumship, the former of which has been quite too common; but now and then we see a man or woman exercise the grand power from a plane of personal purity and goodness, but this cannot be reached where the heart is for long bereft, and that ever is, until the love within goes out to meet as pure a flame.

Black Magic, and low mediumship leads to lost and wrong, and have wrecked many a soul in this day.

White Magic and high mediumship purifies the heart, and sheds abroad the perfume of angels. It teaches selfcontrol – a lesson to be learned by all; it inculcates charity, goodness, forbearance.

Compound or conglomerate mediumship is that state of things wherein the requisite sphere (aura) cannot be furnished in sufficient quantity by any *one* person, but can be from the combined emanation of several; thus it often happens that under good conditions the manifestations take place freely in circles composed of persons no one of whom is mediumistic sufficiently. It also frequently happens that the presence of certain persons will prevent the manifestations even in the presence of strong and first-class media; because such persons either consume, annul or dissipate the media aura.

Where a person alone desires to become a medium, without any assistance from others in the flesh, the individual should provide four thick glass salt-cellars, or the bottoms of broken bottles, or tumblers; in short, anything that is a good electric insulator. The legs of the chair on which the person sits must be placed on these insulators, as also the legs of the foot-stool on which the feet must be placed, while no part of the body or dress should be allowed to touch the floor. The stand or table used by the sitter should also be insulated. Thus prepared the person should select a quiet hour, from sunset to midnight, in which to sit. There should be a mellow, not too bright light burning – candle-lights are best – the face should be turned either North or South, but *never* East or West, because the magnetic flow of the earth is from North to South, the electric from South to North; while the dia magnetic-electric currents invariably cross these lines at right angles, and in their passage disturb and dissipate the medial aura, or "psychic force" and render more difficult the success of the experiment.

The sittings should, if possible, take place at the same hour and locality *every* night, until the hoped-for results follow. But, if circumstances occur to render that impossible, then the person should sit at whatever place the party may happen to be, conforming as far as possible with the rules laid down, nor is it advisable to permit any other person to assist at the sitting after a lone experiment is begun, for the admixture of a new magnetism is almost sure to destroy the conditions already obtained.

The same general rules ought to be followed no matter whether by one person or more, *but* the same ones should always be present, and no more, no less; and they ought always to occupy the same seats at the stand or table. It ought also to be observed that these sittings should always be held in the same room, if possible, an upper chamber, especially devoted to the end sought; for by continued observance of this rule the aura-media is not lost, but in time will so penetrate and permeate the walls and ceiling as to render it a veritable "Spirit Room," wherein results will follow quicker, stronger and better than anywhere else in that house.

The machinery absolutely necessary for successful physical manifestations are:

1st. Harmony, silence, save music, singing and gentle conversation;

2nd. A dark chamber or cabinet;

3rd. Honesty, earnestness, truthfulness, goodness.

4th. Slate-pencils, slate or pencil and paper.

5th. A vial of olive oil.

6th. A looking-glass, or what is far better, a magic mirror or crystal. This, of course, where the Planchette is not used.

If the Planchette is used, then neither pencil or paper nor slate is required. It is well though to have a mirror, crystal or magic glass on the same table as the Planchette.

Such, in brief, is the rationale of mediumship – a fact which, like these of magnetism, is indisputable, and fixed beyond. doubt, cavil or question. By means of these grand facts, the immortality of the soul has been, and is, triumphantly proved. By the concurrent testimony of all the returned dead this other great fact is established, viz: That the post mortem existence *is* a vast improvement on this, and that *life* is one of constant *improvement* and *advancement*, that mankind finds peace, pleasure, rest, labor, usefulness and affectionate friendship, unswerving, incorruptible love.

NOTE. – To develop conscious mediumship, which is the only *safe* mediumship, whether only one desires to develop or six, those undergoing development must never allow themselves to fall into a doze or a sleep, but rather give up the sitting when beginning to feel drowsy. *Bear this in mind.*

Lesson 1

MAGEAN MAGIC
SUPREME COMMAND TO THE DEITIES

On entering upon this course of instructions, lay aside for the time being all previous theories and beliefs. If there is anything you do not understand, do not become antagonistic. Accept the statements as given. As you proceed, the light will shine on your path. The faithful practice of the rules will prove the truth of these statements.

It is taken for granted that you understand the general laws which govern the thought-world. That health, wealth, love, success, all things you desire, are of your own creation. We express for ourselves, in person and environment, whatever we have the power to create. That power is simply the *will* to think consciously along definite lines and to put these thoughts *into deeds and acts*. To have faith and courage to act as we think. In other words, just in the exact image in which we create our thoughts, will be our lives. A continuous holding fast to the thoughts on any subject, *must and will* bring them into objectivity.

We are the creators of our own destiny. No one says "no" to us but ourselves. We do not have to beseech God any more than we have to beseech the sun to shine. The sun shines because it is its law to shine. It cannot help but shine. If it does not shine upon you it is only because you do not come out where it can shine upon you. No more can God help pouring into us wisdom, love, opulence. Nothing can hinder Him but our own thoughts. God wants us to have what we want so long as it is the good and the true, and if we fall short of expressing our desires the fault lies *within* ourselves.

To the earnest student "White Magic" is the *key* to the door of success. But the pupil must *use* the key. The door does not open of itself. It needs perseverance and will to enter boldly and claim your inheritance.

It is a fact, known beyond dispute, that no person can be a success either physically, spiritually or financially unless that person possesses an ample store of what is usually termed animal magnetism, but which is, in fact, spiritual magnetism, from the sun. It is this fact which enables one man or woman to sway a multitude and ultimately carve their name on the Rock of Ages. It is therefore absolutely necessary that each person, unless they were fortunately born with an abundant supply of this vital force, to pursue some method whereby they may acquire it, and the following exercises are designed for that purpose.

Before you begin these exercises salute the four cardinal deities each time, in the following manner, viz:

Stand erect and turn your face towards the East and repeat the name of Jehovah – proncunced Ye-haw – three times;

then turn your face towards the South and three times pronounce the name Adoni – pronounced A-don-i.

Turn to the North in like manner and utter the name Ahih – pronounced Eye-ee.

Then face the West and three times say the name Agla. After you have done so sit down and after meditating for a few minutes upon the wonderful works of the Great Creator repeat the following: "Let all beings be peaceful, let all mankind be happy, let all beings be blissful." Then begin the following exercises:

EXERCISE FOR THE FIRST WEEK

Stand in some quiet place where the air is pure and has been vitalized by the sun, place the right hand in the palm of the left, keep your feet apart so that heels will not touch. Fill the lungs to their utmost capacity and hold the breath four seconds, counting four, exhale very slowly. Repeat by filling the lungs to their fullest capacity and holding the breath five seconds; exhale slowly. Increase to eight seconds. Inhale through nose only.

Practice this deep breathing exercise for five minutes, three times a day for a week, in the morning, before the noon meal, and before retiring at night.

Do not fail in your practice. We purposely make the first three lessons simple, a test of your real desire. If you follow them in word and spirit – the future will open up to you with unnumbered blessings. Have faith that you are now on the path to your own. Have faith that staggers not at appearances; the faith that compels obedience when the command goes out to the sleeper - "Lazarus, come forth!" Faith enables the mind to open the door to everything that the mind desires, and the more we depend upon the power of the mighty soul, the more power we shall receive. Therefore combine faith with these exercises and the largest, most practical, and best results will be yours.

Lesson 2

SUPREME COMMAND TO THE DEITIES

More people fail to achieve success from lack of a definite plan, or system, than from anything else. No matter how much ability one may have, if he lacks in stick-to-it-ive-ness, the very *essence* of success, he will accomplish but little.

Desire, concentration and breath compose the trinity of success. Many systems of development have been taught, but very few of them are effective, because they do not combine these three essentials. They do not know that the great power in accomplishment is the natural sequence of the *conscious breathing* upon a thought form; that breath, as it relates itself to desire and concentration, produce "White Magic."

To illustrate: You may have a desire, not a mere wish but a longing, yearning desire for some one thing that you would objectify in your life. Follow this threefold process.

1. Condense that desire into one word or very short sentence.
2. Visualize it. That is, see yourself in possession of that which you desire; see yourself surrounded by that which you desire. Outline it so clearly in your thought that it stands out boldly; so stamped on your thought-world that it becomes the pattern for objectivity or materialization.
3. Breathe upon it. Inhale slowly, thinking calmly, positively of that thought-picture. Feel that you are drawing in the power to create, the power to accomplish this desire, from the infinite supply. Make the moment of the held breath one of poise, power, expectation. *Breathe out love.*

The law works both ways. You must pay for what you receive. If you take anything from the infinite, you must give its equivalent to humanity. For example:

1. You breathe in the desire for money.
2. Hold breath an instant, feeling vibrant with power.
3. Breathe out love for all humanity.

You establish a balance.

The infinite storehouse is full of unrelated atoms. Every focused thought selects an atom, as it were, and places it in the building of your mental picture. Continued, systematic concentration brings together these atoms. When you realize that the atoms of the unseen side are related to those on the material plane, is it not easy to understand how right thinking produces a corresponding environment?

If you can bring to your assistance a high spiritual exaltation and faith (positive thought force), materialization will soon take place, for faith and exaltation will act as a cement, binding together the atoms of your thought-world.

Remember that constructive, hopeful, positive thought builds your desires into realization; while every destructive, discouraged, negative thought tears down your structure.

The breathing is *all* important. "By carrying a thought on the breath the whole organism is stirred and magnetized to a high degree. The personal currents open and expand, inviting supply. There is lack of nothing in the universal energy; the lack is in ourselves, contracting our own avenues and shutting out supply or concealing the creative power through neglect to visualize the thought, fixing it in the mind and *breathing upon it* as a matrix for manifestation."

EXERCISE FOR SECOND WEEK

Take same position as for first lesson, empty the lungs completely, breathing out every, particle of air possible, then inhale until the lungs are packed full, clasp the hands together and exhale very slowly. Practice this exercise for at least ten minutes, three times a day.

The student may take any thought desired while taking this exercise. Breathe in health, wealth, success or any other thing you desire, hold yourself poised a moment, then slowly breathe out love.

Do not practice these exercises without some definite thought. Vision only the ideal – then trust the soul for the means of accomplishment.

Lesson 3

MAGEAN MAGIC

The links that bind Demand and Supply are Faith and Affirmation. There is tremendous power, genuine creative power in affirming, or asserting a thing. The supply is always equal to the demand – but, the demand must be consciously made *first*. "Thou shalt decree a thing and it shall be."

Affirmations, and especially audible ones, give the faith and self-confidence necessary to accomplish your desires. Persisted in, this self-treatment produces a buoyancy that amounts to positive knowledge and then, no matter what the external conditions are at the time, you *know* that it is yours. You are full of divine attraction – a magnet drawing abundant supply. It literally turns out, that when you ask for one thing, a dozen other things come with it to prove that "creative energy is ready to burst into bloom the moment we make continuous connection with it."

The success a man achieves simply represents his expectations of himself. His environment is the material reflection of his mental picture. The power he uses is nothing more than trained, persistent thought aimed in the direction of the great purpose he has decided to accomplish. "There is no law by which you can achieve success in anything without expecting it, demanding it, assuming it."

Faith is the secret of occult power. It will open the door to every desire. It makes possible the seeming impossible.

"Your wants are impressed on the divine mind only by your faith. Fear or doubt cuts the connection."

"What things so ever you desire, when you pray, *believe* (active faith) that you receive them and then ye shall have them." Read the eleventh chapter of Hebrews, especially verses 32 to 36.

EXERCISE FOR THIRD WEEK

Take same position as before, extend arms toward the South, inhale a deep breath, filling the lungs to the fullest capacity, then clasp the hands together and turn completely around in the same direction as the hands of a clock, face the South and then slowly exhale the breath. Practice in this manner for ten minutes three times a day. If you become dizzy in turning around, pause for a moment. Remember to always salute the four cardinal points.

It is wise at this point to acquaint the student with a method whereby he may be able to kill fear instantly, for no man has ever made a financial success by his own effort who was afflicted by fear. Inhale a full breath, filling the lungs and abdomen first, then expanding the lungs and upper chest. Now force the air out of the chest into the abdomen, expanding it to the fullest extent, then draw the abdomen in again, forcing the air back into the chest. Repeat this process several times before expelling the breath. Practice this exercise several times a day. It will kill fear.

In parting: The person who entertains the Ordinary thought will *never* become extra-ordinary.

Lesson 4

MAGEAN MAGIC

On a famous sun-dial is written this motto – one worth adopting for life: "I record none but hours of sunshine." How beautiful beyond words would your life be if tuned to this key of brightness.

Too much cannot be said about the use and abuse of the thought-world. If you would have a bright, happy environment you must hold bright, happy, *definite* thoughts in your mind. Thoughts are not only things, but things are thoughts.

You have not learned the art of living until you have trained yourself to register only the constructive thought. So long as one demoralizing wave of thought has the power to possess you, you are in bondage. All suffering, sickness, poverty and failure, is the result of this bondage. There is no permanent or *real* outward way to escape from failure or unhappiness. All must come from within. Success or victory must be won in your own soul first, and then you need not worry or try to help in the outer demonstration. "The very walls of Jericho which keep you from your desire must fall before you."

Take these two sentences – repeat them over and over until they become a part of you:

"Success comes to you according to the persistent desire and positive expectation you put into it," and

"How can I lack any good, since mind is causation and I can think as I please."

EXERCISE FOR FOURTH WEEK

This exercise is practiced by the Yogi of India and is one of the greatest secrets of their art, whereby their minds are kept strong and their bodies free from disease.

Sit perfectly upright. The spinal cord, although it is inside the vertebral column, is not attached to it. If you sit crooked you disturb the spinal cord, so let it be free. You do yourself an injury trying to meditate in a crooked posture. The three parts of the body must be held straight; the chest, the neck and the head in one line. You will find that by a little practice this will come just as easy as breathing.

The next thing is to concentrate your mind upon the fact that disease is an enemy, and that by breathing in the spirit of life, which is God, you can drive out the (d)evil, which is disease.

Slowly fill the lungs with breath through the left nostril, and at the same time concentrate your mind upon some sacred word, such as the word Jehovah, then hold the spirit or breath in your lungs for some time, then slowly exhale it through the right nostril. This you will find a little difficult at first to practice. The easiest way is to stop the right nostril with the thumb, and then slowly draw in the breath through the left, then close both nostrils with the thumb and forefinger and set your mind upon the fact that you are driving out disease, and then take the thumb off and let the breath out through the right nostril.

Next inhale slowly through the left nostril, keeping the right closed by the forefinger, and then close as before.

The way the Hindu's practice this would be difficult for our people and of no advantage. It is well to begin with four seconds and slowly increase : draw in four seconds, hold sixteen, then throw out in eight and hold out eight seconds. Five minutes each day is sufficient to practice this last exercise until you become accustomed.

After you have faithfully followed the instructions as given above, you will begin to feel a wonderful exhiliration fill your whole being. Your eyes will grow bright and clear, the weak, tired feeling will have left your body and, in short, you will feel as if you could lift yourself up by the power of a thought.

You are now in condition to receive knowledge from the great thought force that pervades the whole universe, and in order to do this, sit down in a quiet, easy posture, with the spinal column erect, with your face toward the East, because that is the center from which the spiritual wisdom of the universe flows, from the root of the tree of knowledge. Have the room slightly darkened, close the eyes, sit in this manner about twenty minutes at high twelve each day and soon you will have knowledge come to you that you cannot obtain from any other source and the most difficult problems will suddenly unfold before you like the petals of a flower.

CAUTION – After you have once begun the above exercise, do not, under any circumstances, have any intercourse for the mere pleasure of it, as the loss of the vital fluid will prevent the highest development. Those wishing to reach the highest should get "Divine Alchemy," and follow *the* law.

Lesson 5

HOW TO OBTAIN FINANCIAL SUCCESS

"Seek and ye shall find, knock (demand) and it shall be opened unto you." This is true in a material sense just the same as in a spiritual sense. Man is an exact counterpart of the universe, and every part of him is connected therewith, and when he once knows where and how he is so connected he is able to draw from the forces of nature just exactly what he wants.

All occult work is based upon the *concentration* of the mind. By use of will-power we draw to ourselves just what we may demand through the understanding of the laws governing these things. The result of *this* method is determined by the amount of knowledge we possess by which our *faith* becomes great, for then the supply will be in accord with the demand.

The law of correspondence applied to concentration by demand reveals our relationship to the four great centers: North, South, East and West. The North represents the mineral world, the center or kingdom from which we draw all material wealth, money, success and prosperity. Its nature, like the mineral kingdom, is cold, unfeeling, devoid of warmth and life, but holds in its grasp that material which most of us are constantly toiling for, that we may supply the physical needs. We are related to this center by our bone and muscular system, for the mineral kingdom is to the physical structure of the earth what our bone system is to the physical body; thus the law of correspondence gives us the relationship or wires of connection to this special kingdom and when we recognize the real self and its powers we have but to face the center which represents this kingdom and demand our own. Development at this center is acquisition of wealth, mineral psychometry. The color is red and represents force and strength on a dense material plane. Make all your demands between the new moon and the full moon.

By following the above advice you will find that you will obtain much better results for the reason that when it is on the increase we all receive the benefit of its vibrations and it is directly contrary when it is on the decrease. By consulting your Bible you will find that Moses and all the Jewish priests who came after him were close observers of the various phases of the moon and governed themselves thereby.

DEMAND FOR WEALTH

Face the North and say: "O, King of the North, I demand of thee my own." Repeat this demand nine times, making a slight pause after each demand. Make your demands at twelve o'clock at noon or as soon thereafter as possible or at low twelve at night. Make all your demands in a firm and decided tone of voice.

If you are about to enter into a business deal with any person, make your demands as above directed; then determine in your own mind just what position you intend to take in the matter and what you expect to accomplish; form a mental picture of the person with whom you are about to deal, provided he is not personally known to you, then begin and make your demands of him as if he were really present. Say to him in a firm tone: You must do as I say – say what you want them to do (mentally) in words *positive*, but short. Feel confident that you do and will accomplish your wish. *Do not doubt*; thought is creation, vibration, dominating, and it will go where you send it, and perform its *mission*, if done in harmony with this law.

Always shake hands, if possible, for it will help you to impress your wish upon his mind. When shaking hands with any one whom you wish to impress or influence, press your finger in the palm of their hand and your thumb upon the outside, just over the third finger, and mentally make the same suggestion you made in your room.

When making any business deal with another person never sit down so that they will be above you, for by so doing their influence becomes stronger, and never turn your back or side to the other party for then you become negative. Face your party squarely; look him squarely in the eyes; talk to him in a firm, decided way and don't be afraid to express your real self. Don't be afraid to use the word no, when it is necessary.

Lesson 6

THE SOUTH CENTER

This center corresponds to the vegetable world or kingdom of life and vigorous health.

We are related to it by the vascular system, our cords and ligaments. We face this center, and while recognizing the power of the sun, we draw into our bodies the breath, the thought, the element of life that builds up our bodies and makes them fit temples for the soul.

The psychic developments gained at this center are physical clairvoyance and vegetable psychometry and clairvoyance. Yellow is the color which symbolizes this center. It represents the life of the tropics, fruits and flowers and is an emblem of sunshine.

DEMAND FOR SOUTH CENTER

Facing South, say: "O wonderful planet Sun, giving to the earth warmth and vigor, I would draw from thee through this center, life, health and vigor until my body is a fit temple for the soul", then, "O Sun, give out to others life abundant." Repeat nine times as at first directed. Make this demand at high twelve.

If any of your friends or family are sick make your demands as follows: "O Gabriel, Michael, Raphael and Uriel, who represent and guard over the Sun, Moon, Mercury and Venus, I ask with all earnestness that you restore to health (name the person). This I ask in the name of the great Adony who hath created and watches over all. Ah-um."

THE EAST CENTER

The East represents the mental kingdom upon which depends the spirituality of the race. Its color is blue and signifies spirit and intellect on this plane. Development at the East center is spiritual clairvoyance, inspirational speaking and writing, painting and all development belonging to the realm of art. Before making the demand at this center, if you like, burn a little incense composed of the following: pulverized myrrh, white rosin and sulphur, one ounce each; common salt, one-quarter ounce; mix. The effect is to exalt the soul faculties,

DEMAND FOR THE EAST CENTER

Facing East, say: "I demand the power of mentality and spirituality that I may overcome all conditions of matter." Repeat nine times, then read Psalm 121.

THE WEST CENTER

The West represents the activity of the people, denoting the restlessness which develops and gives us all manner of civilization. Demand at this center should be made when dealing with people.

DEMAND FOR WEST CENTER

Facing the West, say: "I demand that (naming the individual) shall (here state what you wish done)." Repeat nine times. Remember that the results of your demands will depend upon the *will* and *faith* you exert when you make them and the earnestness of your purpose.

Always accompany your demands by the very best efforts on your part. God helps these who make an effort to help themselves. Never make your demands when in an angry or agitated frame of mind. In fact, a good occultist never allows himself to become angry as it destroys his equilibrium. Make your demands in your own private room and always keep that filled with fresh air and sunlight and you will, at last, penetrate the nine brilliant arches and see the beautiful triangle with the ineffable name written thereon.

NOTE – A secret known to but few. Use freely the perfume of the wild wood violet, just the same as you would any other perfume. You will find that it will be a great aid to you in making friends, especially of the opposite sex. If you add carnation pink you will find that it has quite a hypnotic effect both upon yourself and others with whom you may come in contact.

THE MAGIC WAND

Choose the wood of an almond or hazel tree which has flowers for the first time; cut it off at one blow with a sharp knife which has never before been used.

Through this bore a small hole from end to end and insert a magnetized steel needle of the same length. One end is then to be closed by a clear glass bead and the other end by a bead of rosin. Each end is then covered with silk which is fastened by a ring at each end.

One ring must be fitted near each end, these must be flat and broad enough so as to allow engraving upon them. One of them is to be of zinc and the other of brass.

Each of these rings is to have two small holes to which are fastened two chains, one of brass and the other of zinc. These chains must be wound around the band.

Upon the wand must be written the names of the twelve spirits of the zodiacal cycle, or rather, their sigils should be written on it.

The illustration will give you a clear idea of how this is to be done, with the exception that the chains are not shown.

No other work contains the true secret of making this wand as these instructions are taken from the only original manuscript known to exist and it is the only genuine method.

ŚARACHIEL ARAZIEL ŚARRAIEL PHAKIEL
SERATIEL ŚCHALTIEL CHADAKIEL ŚARTZIEL
ŚARITIEL ŚEMAQIEL TZÁKMAQIEL VACÁBIEL

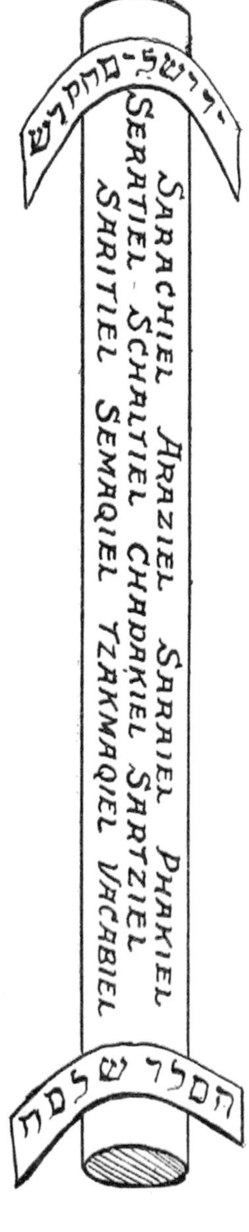

Magic Wand

BOOK SECOND

In the making of the talismans it must be remembered that they are to be made only when four aspects are favorable. The brothers will be taught when this is by private letters at the beginning of each year.

TALISMAN OF INDIA

This figure is a Hindoo talisman much worn by the Brahmins of high caste. There is the lighted torch of long life; the Eastern knife dagger as protection against enemies; the cup of plenty and the ring for domestic happiness; at the foot lie the tiger and the cow, a symbol of peace.

This is much valued by all classes of Hindoos and is considered a strong talisman for peace, goodwill, domestic happiness, and success. Especially agricultural success. It is best engraved on silver, but can be engrossed upon parchment and worn in a silk bag on the breast.

Cut 1

TALISMANS FOR JANUARY

The Traveller's Friend (2)

TALISMANS FOR JANUARY

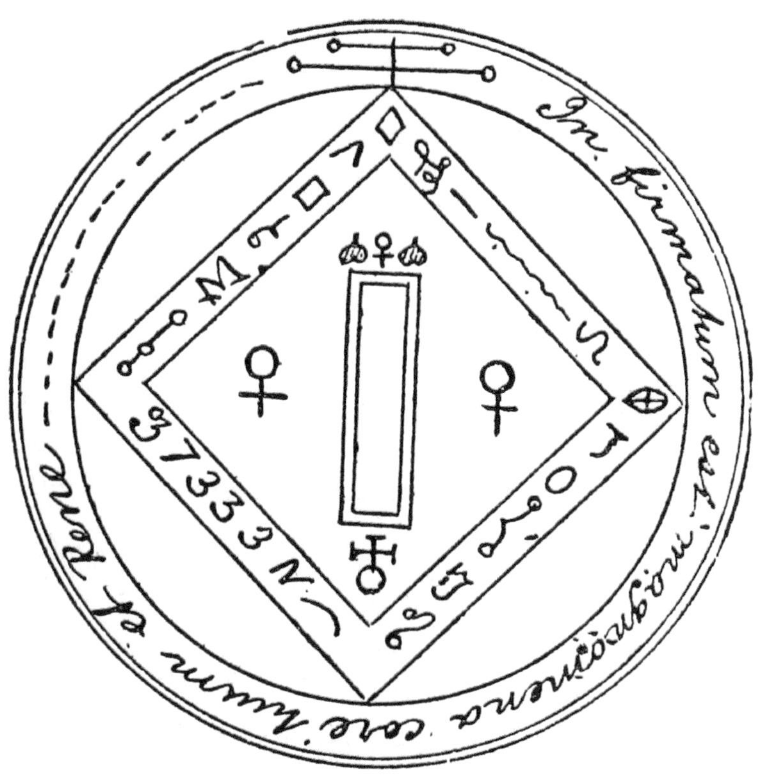

Woman's Love (3)

A grand pentacle or talisman of Rabbi Solomon, the Great King,

TALISMANS FOR FEBRUARY

Against Oppression (4)

TALISMANS FOR FEBRUARY

Trade (5)

TALISMANS FOR MARCH

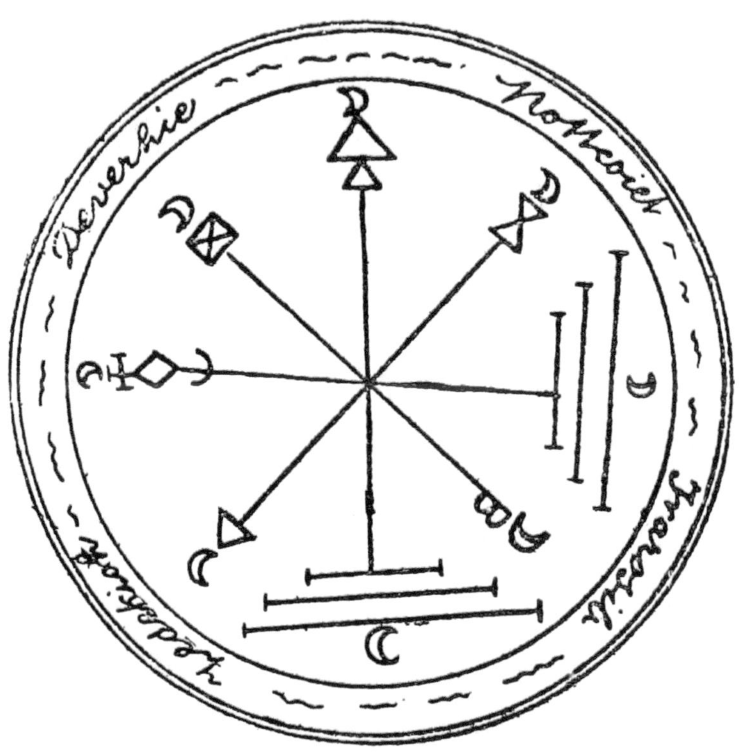

The Miner's Friend (6)

TALISMANS FOR MARCH

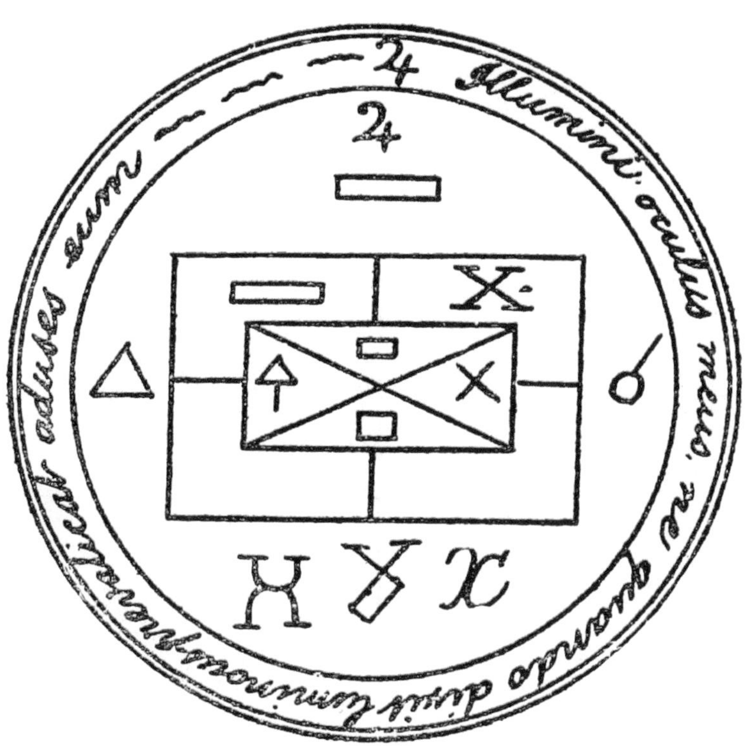

Hazards (7)

TALISMANS FOR APRIL

Jupiter, Talisman for all good (8)

TALISMANS FOR APRIL

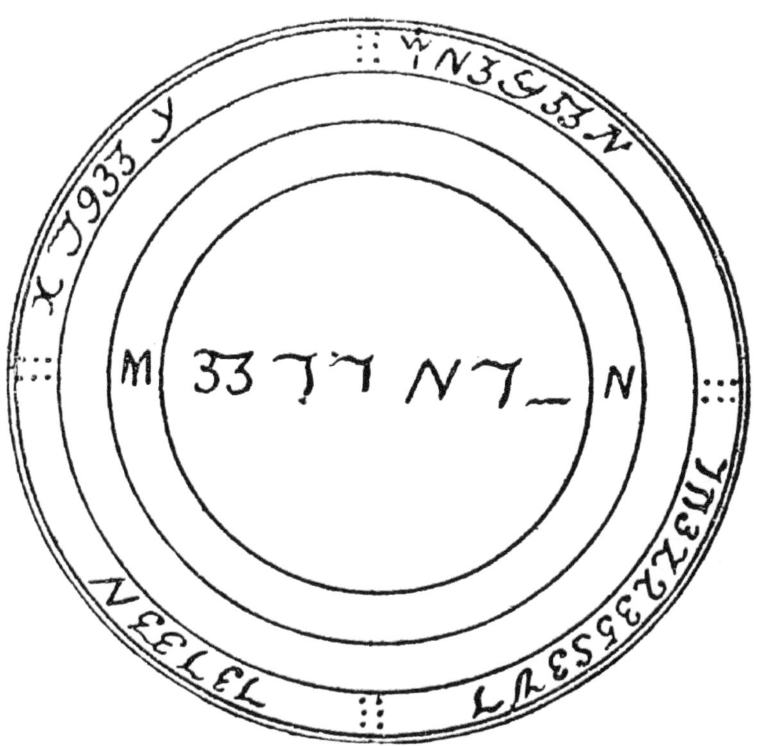

Prosperity (9)

TALISMANS FOR MAY

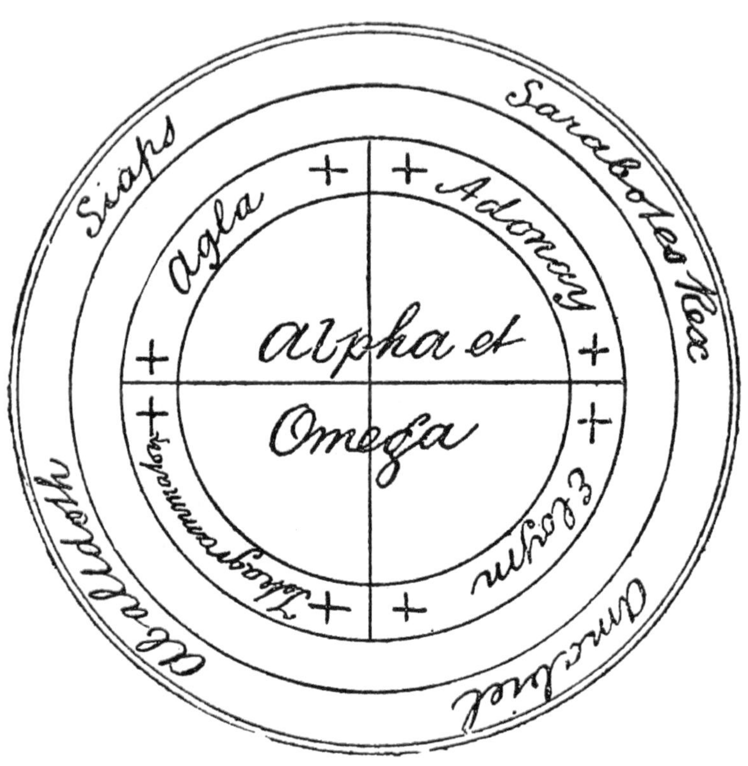

Venus, for all good (10)

TALISMANS FOR MAY

Health (11)

TALISMAN FOR JUNE

Mercury, the Ruler of the Month (12)

EARLY CHRISTIAN PHYLACTERY

The Grand Pentacle or Talisman for Peace and Love (13)

A charm or talisman which was worn by the early Christians.

TALISMAN FOR JULY

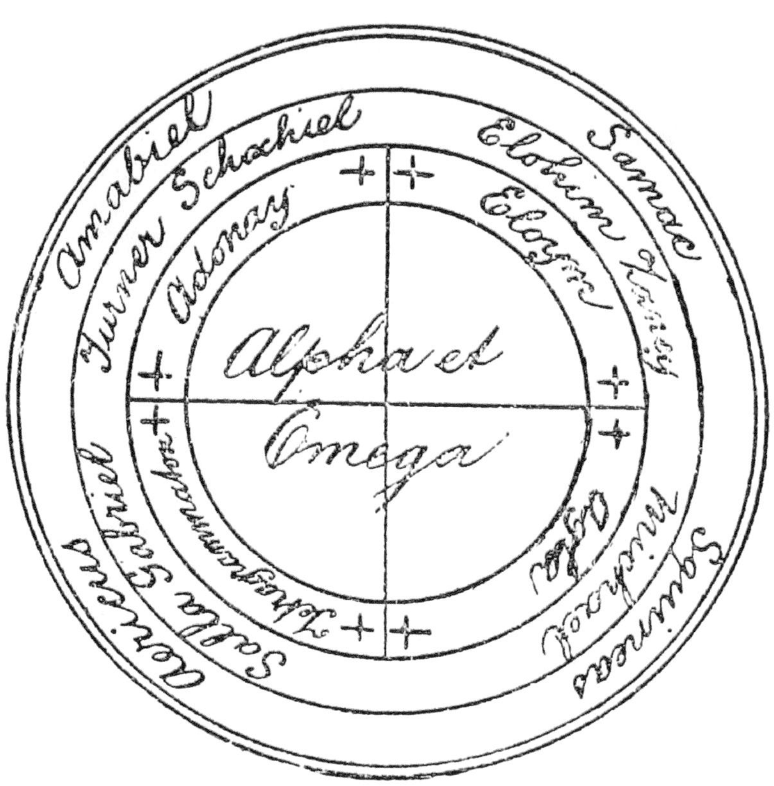

Mars, Ruler of the Month (14) Warrior's Friend

TALISMAN FOR JULY

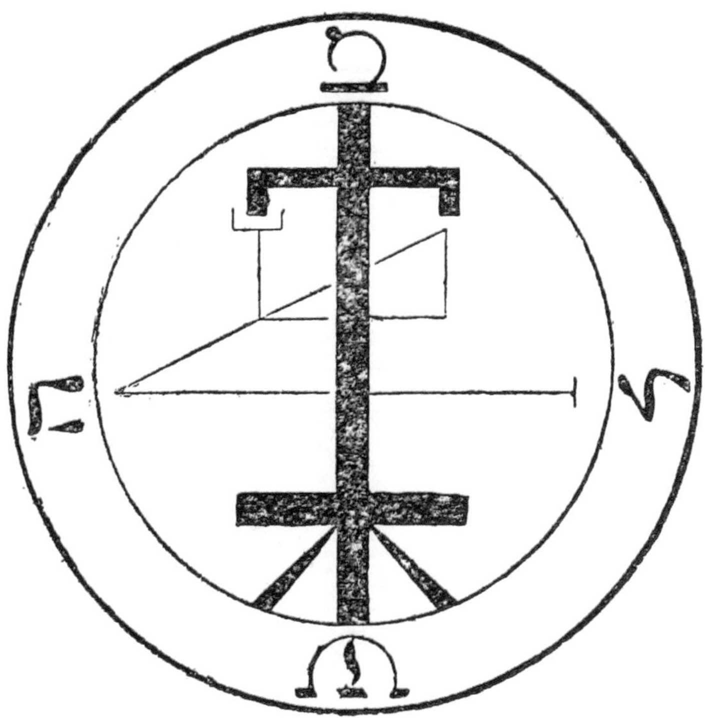

The grand Pentacle or Talisman to bring Peacefulness (15)

The Pentagram of the Magic Blazing Star of the children of Hiram. To each of its points a ray of light ascends and from each a ray goes forth. The magnetic influence issues in two trains from the head, from either hand and from either foot. This represents the spirit of order and illustrates the circulating law of lightning.

TALISMANS FOR AUGUST

Sun, Talisman against disease (16)

TALISMANS FOR AUGUST

The Grand Pentacle or Talisman of Orion (17) an early Crusader's Talisman

St. Michael (or Orion) doing battle with the Serpent or Dragon. For a Crusader, Knight Templar or *traveller* to carry this sign and turn to it in time of weakness, great strength and courage shall come to him and he shall conquer his enemies.

TALISMANS FOR SEPTEMBER

Saturn, Talisman against Evil (18)

TALISMANS FOR SEPTEMBER

III-Wishing and Acts of Enemies (19)

TALISMANS FOR OCTOBER

Success and Long Life (20)

TALISMANS FOR OCTOBER

Rabbi Solomon, success in All Things (21)

TALISMANS FOR NOVEMBER

Health, Wealth and Happiness (22)

TALISMANS FOR NOVEMBER

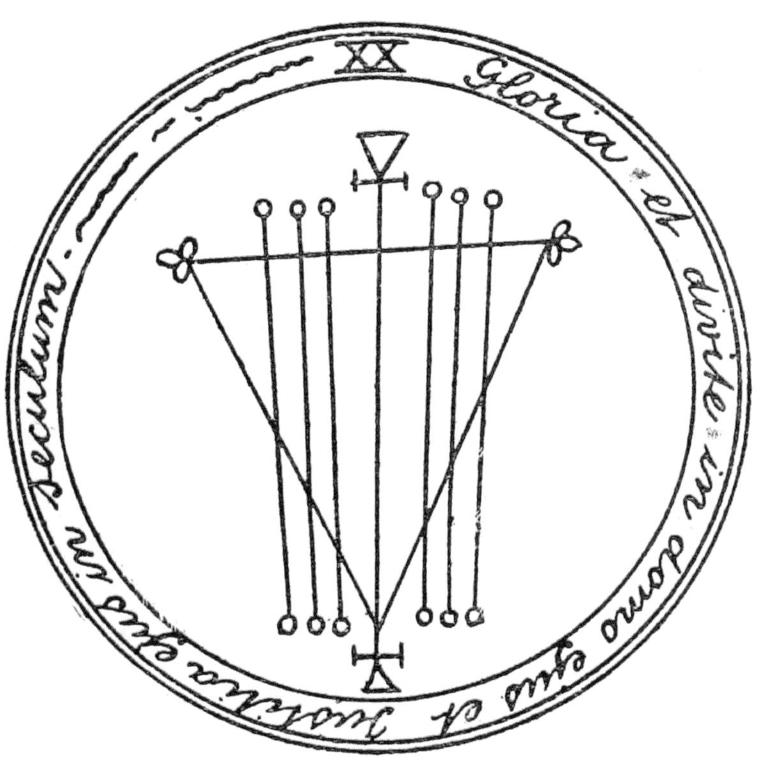

Honor, Riches (23)

TALISMANS FOR DECEMBER

Holy Sigils of the Names of God.

The front part. The Back part.

The Holy Signals, against Disease and for Happiness (24)

TALISMANS FOR DECEMBER

Man's Love (25)

ORDER OF THE OLD MAN OF THE PYRAMID

Inner Mysteries of the *Comte de Gabalis.*

These talismans are amongst the easiest to make since they can be made on the cheaper metals or upon silk. Each talisman has a ring, the characters found below the ring should be engraved on the inner side of the ring.

Cut a.

The talisman and ring of Cut a should be worn when the Neophyte desires to come into communication with the Celestial or Invisible Brotherhood. It will help to place him or her into harmonicus vibration with the invisible order and also prevent the obsession of evil spirits. The talisman should be engraven on silver or embroidered upon sky-blue satin. The ring should be made of silver.

Cut b.

Talisman and ring of Cut b is wholly for obtaining harmonious condition between loved ones, between husband and wife, between sweethearts and friends. It is only for the male sex. The talisman should be of silver or on black satin, and work privately. The ring also of silver. It is not necessary that both be worn at one time. These talismans may also be worn in the secret room while the student is undergoing spiritual development as they will place the Neophyte in harmony with the spirits which are of violet aura, that of the soul.

Cut c.

A talisman or ring which should be worn by those seeking treasures of the earth, such as gold, silver, copper, etc. The talisman should be made of gold, or gold thread used to embroider the design upon green satin. The ring is to be of gold.

Cut d.

Talisman d is of especial value to those who would become seers, whether through clairvoyance, spiritualism, etc. It is a help to produce the vibrations necessary to bring about the state which helps the soul to penetrate the invisible or distance. The talisman should be of violet satin, embroidered with silver thread. The ring should be of silver and worn upon left hand.

Cut e.

Talisman e is of especial value for overcoming enemies and also to gain possession of desired secrets. For this reason they must be worn when in the presence of the enemy or those whose secrets may be desired. The talisman should be of gold colored satin and embroidered with gold thread. The ring of gold and worn on little finger of left hand.

Cut f.

Talisman f is to give great help in the accomplishment of any achievement or work that the possessor wishes to undertake. The talisman should be of lilac satin embroidered in shaded silk. The ring may be of silver, or any other costly metal.

Cut g.

Talisman g is for protection from all accident. It should be embroidered with silver thread upon poppy-red satin. The ring can be of silver or gold.

Cut h.

Talisman h is of value to come into touch with the Invisible Brotherhood and helps the wearer to see them in the mirror or crystal or through materialization. It should be of yellow satin, embroidered with black silk. The ring of silver or gold and worn on right hand.

Cut i.

Talisman i is to be worn either as a protection against accidents in travel or as a help to produce proper vibration while practicing the drills for development. It is to be brownish colored satin, embroidered with gold thread. The ring of gold or silver.

Cut j.

Talisman j is for finding all things that may have been hidden and is therefore of value to the seeker after either earthly or spiritual treasures. Talisman is to be of deep blue satin, embroidered with silver thread. Ring of silver.

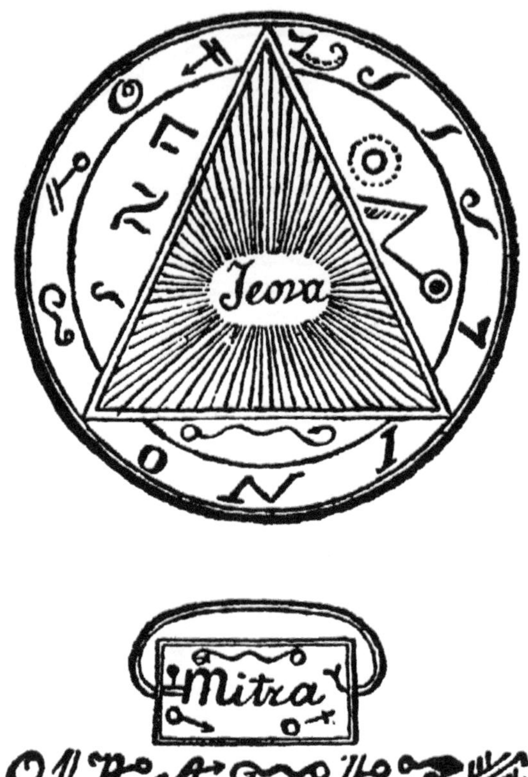

Cut k.

Talisman k is of value only to these who would develop clairaudence or clear-hearing; is to be of light gray satin, embroidered with gold thread. Ring is to be of gold.

Cut 1.

Talisman 1 is for the protection against the influence of all evil spirits and obsessions. It is to be of rose colored satin, embroidered with silver thread. The ring of silver. The ring is to be worn upon the middle finger of the right hand.

Cut m.

Talisman m is for those who desire to be good, true and virtuous but who find temptations too strong. Such should wear a talisman like m, made of saffron colored satin, embroidered with silver thread or a ring made of silver.

Cut n.

Talisman n is to be worn by those who would become experts in the study of minerals and vegetables. Is of special value to the farmer, the mineralogist and also those who would study medicine. It is of great value to the healer. The talisman is made of orange colored satin, embroidered with silver thread. The ring of silver. Both the talisman and ring to be worn in a locket upon breast.

Cut o.

Talisman o is for those who handle ferocious animals, hunters and others who make it a business or pleasure to handle wild animals. The talisman is to be of deep green satin, embroidered with gold. The ring of gold.

Cut p.

Talisman p helps those who would become character readers, those who study human nature and all these studies which have to do with human characteristics. It is made of black satin, embroidered with gold. The ring is to be of gold. The ring is worn on the little finger of right hand.

Cut q.

Talisman q is the greatest known talisman for all who would study the arts and professions. It gives harmonious help or vibrations towards all profound knowledge. It is to be of white satin, embroidered with black silk. The ring of either gold or silver.

Cut r.

Talisman r to be worn by all those who play games of chance, no matter what their nature. The talisman is to be of cerise colored satin, embroidered with both gold and silver thread. The ring can be of gold or silver. The talisman must be worn upon the left arm and fastened with white ribbon. The ring is worn upon little finger of the right hand.

Cut s.

Talisman s is for all those who have enemies and who are forced to fight them. Also those who fear evil spirits. The talisman is made of grayish satin and embroidered with shaded silk. The ring of silver.

Cut t.

Talisman t for those who fear being attacked by any evil, no matter of what nature. The talisman is made of red satin with the center embroidered with gold thread, the border in silver and the figures in black and white silk. It should be worn upon the breast. The ring is to be of either gold or silver and worn on the little finger of left hand.

GRAND ORIENTAL TEMPLE

FIRST DEGREE.

Password "ML"

Foreword to Students.

Warning, Magic, 1st Mystery.

Cells, Organs, etc.

Elementary Astrology.

SECOND DEGREE.

Password "GL"

Warning.

Vibrations, Notes.

Temple of Man, Law of Creation.

Auriferous Clavicle, Five Methods of Influence.

Harmonic Vibration, Including Touch, etc.

Breathing: Astral Plane.

Higher Astrology.

THIRD DEGREE.

Password "SL"

Clavis of Solomon.

Instruments.

Tables of Angels for Sunday.

Fasting Three Days.

FOURTH DEGREE.

Password "RL"

Talismans.

Oration, Conjuration and Invocation for Everybody.

Tables of Angels for Mondny.

Fasting Seven Days.

FIFTH DEGREE.

Password "CL"

Pentacle of the Sun; Oration, Invocation and Conjuration.

Pentacles and Talismans for Sunday and Explanation.

Cabalistic Names of Hours of Day and Night.

Drawings.

Tables of Angels for Tuesday.

Fasting Ten Days.

SIXTH DEGREE.

Password "AL"

Pentacle of the Moon: Oration, Invocation Conjuration.

Pentacle and Talisman for Monday.

Drawings.

Tables of Angels for Wednesday.

Fasting Fourteen Days.

SEVENTH DEGREE.

PASSWORD "ARG"

Pentacle of Mars and Tuesday: Oration, Invocation and Conjuration.

Drawings.

Table of Angels for Thursday.

Fasting Twenty-one Days.

EIGHTH DEGREE.

PASSWORD "MICHAEL"

Pentacles under Mercury for Monday: Oration, Invocation and Conjuration.

Pentacle and Talismans for Wednesday.

Drawings.

Table of Angels for Friday.

Fasting Twenty-eight Days.

NINTH DEGREE.

PASSWORD "GABRIEL"

Pentacle for Thursday under Jupiter: Oration and Conjuration.

Observations on Talismans.

Drawings.

Table of Angels for Saturday.

Fasting Thirty Days.

TENTH DEGREE.

Password "SAMAEL"

Pentacle of Friday under Venus: Oration, Invocation and Conjuration.

Drawings.

Fastings Thirty-five Days.

ELEVENTH DEGREE.

Password "RAPHAEL"

Pentacles of Saturday and Saturn: Oration, Invocation and Conjuration.

Drawings.

Fasting Forty Days.

TWELFTH DEGREE.

Password "CASSIEL"

Mystic Tables, Seals and Characters.

Fasting.

THIRTEENTH DEGREE.

Password "ANAEL"

Angels of Hours of day and night of the Week.

Evocations by Keys of Solomon (Part ii.)

Consecrations and Benedictions of Circle.

Benediction of Perfumes.

Exorcism of Fire upon which Perfumes are to be put.

Exorcism of Spirits of the Air.

Elementals.

FOURTEENTH DEGREE.

Password "MASTER"

Conjuration of Lord's Day.

" of Monday.

" of Tuesday.

" of Wednesday.

" of Thursday.

" of Friday.

" of Saturday.

Considerations of Monday.

" of Tuesday.

" of Wednesday

" of Thursday.

" of Friday.

" of Saturday.

Sacred Seal.

MONTHS, RULING PLANETS AND INCENSE

MONTH.	RULING PLANET.	INSENSE.
March 21 to April 19	Mars	Lignum Aloes
April 20 to May 20	Venus	Saffron
May 21 to June 20	Mercury	Cinnamon
June 21 to July 22	Moon	Myrtle
July 23 to Aug. 22	Sun	Mastic
Aug. 23 to Sept. 22	Mercury	Cinnamon
Sept. 23 to Oct. 22	Venus	Saffron
Oct. 23 to Nov. 21	Mars	Lignum Aloes
Nov. 22 to Dec. 21	Jupiter	Nutmeg
Dec. 22 to Jan. 19	Saturn	Pepper-wort
Jan. 20 to Feb. 18	Uranus	aa*
Feb. 19 to March 20	Neptune	aa*

* aa. For these two a combination of the Seven Aromatics may be used, or the Incense given in "Magean Magic."

The Incense given in "Magean Magic" may be used in the Conjurations or Invocations at all times instead of the Aromatics.

The historical context surrounding the publication of The Grand Grimore

The Grand Grimore, authored by Reuben Swinburne Clymer under the pseudonym "Pythagoras 38," is an eclectic occult training manual intended for lodge members. (It is crucial not to confuse this work with the medieval *Grand Grimoire.*)

This unique occult volume, published in 1910, incorporates material from various classic grimoires, magical evocation rituals, and other occult practices, such as instructions on using the planchette, imagination magic, and breathing exercises.

Notably, *The Grand Grimore* holds a special place in Americana literature, as it emerged during a significant period in American history when the occult movement experienced a surge, primarily influenced by the groundwork laid by Paschal Beverly Randolph. This movement found its foothold in Masonic and new Rosicrucian organizations, shaping a new occult movement in 20th-century America.

Paschal Beverly Randolph

The modern Rosicrucian movement in the United States draws significant inspiration from American Freemasonry, even though it asserts its roots in mystical and alchemical texts published in seventeenth-century Germany.

In the late nineteenth-century it was Paschal Beverly Randolph (1825-1875) who stood out as the most influential Rosicrucian thinker. Despite his mixed race heritage, Randolph achieved remarkable success, garnering a significant following both in Europe and the United States. Randolph's *Magia Sexualis* for example influenced the famous Czech magician Franz Bardon.

Paschal Beverly Randolph was an American medical doctor, occultist, spiritualist, trance medium, and writer, who holds a notable place in history. He is recognized as one of the early individuals to introduce the principles of *erotic alchemy* to North America, and is credited by A. E. Waite with establishing the earliest known Rosicrucian order in the United States.

Born in New York City, Randolph's background is intriguing as he was a free black man with ancestral ties to William Randolph. His mother, Flora Beverly, hailed from a diverse heritage of English, French, German, Native American, and African roots. Tragically, Randolph experienced homelessness and poverty following his mother's early demise, prompting him to seek a livelihood at sea.

During his youth and early adulthood, Randolph's maritime occupations allowed him to traverse vast distances, immersing himself in various cultures and encountering occultists in England and Paris. His keen interest in mysticism and the occult led him to study with local practitioners and explore different religions.

Alongside his work as a trance medium, Randolph pursued medical training and authored numerous books on topics ranging from health and sexuality to spiritualism and occultism. Notably, he fearlessly advocated for birth control when it was largely forbidden to broach such subjects.

In 1858, Randolph founded the *Fraternitas Rosae Crucis*, using the pseudonym "The Rosicrucian" for his spiritual and occult writings. The organization's first lodge was established in San Francisco in 1861, making it the oldest Rosicrucian organization in the United States. While the Fraternitas Rosae Crucis no longer emphasizes Randolph's interest in sex magic, his magico-sexual theories and practices heavily influenced the teachings of the *Hermetic Brotherhood of Luxor*, although there is uncertainty about Randolph's personal association with the Brotherhood. Despite working independently, Randolph's extensive exploration of esoteric teachings solidified his identity as a Rosicrucian.

Paschal Beverly Randolph

Reuben Swinburne Clymer
In 1902, R. Swinburne Clymer (1878–1966) from Quakertown, Pennsylvania, published an historical account of the Rosicrucian movement. Clymer became a prominent American occultist and served from 1922 untill his death in 1966 as the modern Rosicrucian Supreme Grand Master of the FRC (Fraternitas Rosae Crucis), founded by Randolph. In the years before, he also established his own Rosicrucian Fraternity, adopting a hierarchical structure reminiscent of Freemasonry. Within this organization, the *Imperialistic Council and Venerable Order of the Magi* held authority, while individuals could progress through various degrees such as *Priests of Melchizedek*, *Knights of Chivalry*, and the *Order of the Holy Grail*.

Clymer pursued medical studies in Chicago, eventually becoming a registered osteopath in New York in 1910. However, his involvement in alternative medicine frequently brought him into opposition with the United States government and the American Medical Association (AMA). Clymer operated the "International Academy of the Natural and Sacred Science" in Union City, Michigan, where a correspondence course on the "Natural System of Healing" was offered. As an osteopath, Clymer was an outspoken opponent of vaccination and asserted that meat consumption, particularly when combined with beans, bread, potatoes, and beer, was the primary cause of cancer, immorality, and insanity. He promoted a pescatarian diet, advocating for the exclusion of red meat, which he considered toxic. His dietary beliefs were reflected in various publications, including *The Rose Cross Aid Cook Book* authored by Clara Witt and Clymer's own work titled *Diet: The Way to Health.*

Throughout his life, Clymer kept an admiration for his predecessor Paschal Beverly Randolph. Clymer established his Philosophical Publishing Company in either 1900 or 1904, through which he preserved Randolph's writings and created a hagiographic (though largely fictitious) history of him. He attributed the foundation of his occult orders to Randolph, despite their largely unrelated origins, connecting various *Hermetic Brotherhood of Light*-orders in Quakertown to Randolph's lineage.

Clymer crafted a more cohesive belief system based on Randolph's thoughts, refining some of the problematic sex magic practices associated with Randolph and addressing his self-contradictions on numerous points. The fictional history Clymer constructed, portrayed Randolph as the legitimate heir of an ancient Rosicrucian tradition in America. This fabrication involved connecting Randolph's "order" to historical figures like Abraham Lincoln, Napoleon III, Alexandre Saint-Yves d'Alveydre, Papus, Albert Pike, and the Count of St. Germain, as well as to ancient Egyptian Rosicrucians, creating an elaborate pseudo-history. Although Clymer genuinely believed his biography of Randolph to be historically accurate, it is now recognized as largely fictional.

Rosicrucian Rivalry

Clymer was passionately involved in various fields, including the esoteric arts, and authored numerous works on subjects ranging from alchemy and nutrition to religion, sex magic, and spiritualism. However, his pursuits often resulted in conflicts with figures and institutions. Clymer's assertion of his position as the authentic leader of American Rosicrucianism pulled him into a long-lasting conflict with Harvey Spencer Lewis, the founder of the AMORC (Ancient Mystical Order Rosae Crucis). This rivalry escalated into bitter contention due to their contrasting beliefs regarding the role of sex in magic. Each side accused the other of promoting perverse teachings while staunchly defending their practices as enlightened and pure.

Clymer's perspectives, heavily influenced by Randolph's teachings, centered on the regular exchange of bodily fluids between married partners as a crucial element for the physical and spiritual well-being of each individual. Clymer and Lewis also engaged in a competition for the recognition and affiliation of different national branches of the OTO (Ordo Templi Orientis), both achieving comparable success without gaining the upper hand to claim legitimacy over each other. In 1934, Lewis co-founded FUDOSI (Fédération Universelle des Ordres et Sociétés Initiatiques), which acknowledged AMORC as the true heirs of American Rosicrucianism. In response, Clymer co-founded FUDOFSI (Fédération Universelle des Ordres, Fraternités et Sociétés Initiatiques) in 1938, alongside Constant Chevillon and Jean Bricaud, supporting his FRC. Clymer denounced Lewis's FUDOSI, considering it an unsuccessful attempt at legitimization.

The rivalry intensified, with AMORC publishing material criticizing Clymer's ideas as "some of the weirdest notions that a human mind ever harbored" and highlighting his "self-appointed and self-devised" positions. And it must be said that Clymer provided a lot of free ammunition for his opponent by uttering statements that were quite "unusual," even in occult circles. For example, he translated the famous work

'Clymer was passionately involved in various fields, including the esoteric arts, and authored numerous works on subjects ranging from alchemy and nutrition to religion, sex magic, and spiritualism.'

on incubi and succubi of Ludovico Maria Sinistrari but changed Sinistrari's incubi and succubi to Elementals and suggested that the virgin birth of Jesus was the result of a Salamander impregnating Mary.

Clymer retaliated by raising suspicions about Lewis's doctorate, accusing him of promoting inauthentic works and practicing black magic due to his association with Aleister Crowley. Crowley initially offered to assist Lewis in countering Clymer's attacks, but their later dispute over control of AMORC led to a rift between them. This intense American rivalry eventually reverberated in European Rosicrucianism, creating divisions within the community.

In 1914, a resurgence of interest in Rosicrucianism occurred during the tercentenary celebration of the original Rosicrucian manifesto. Subsequently, in 1915, H. Spencer Lewis founded the Ancient Mystical Order Rosae Crucis (AMORC), which drew inspiration from Theosophy and the Golden Dawn. Initially established in New York, Lewis later embraced the prevailing trend of esoteric groups moving westward, eventually making California the global hub of the New Age movement. By 1918, he had relocated to San Francisco, and in 1927, the world headquarters for AMORC was established in San Jose. This transformative period significantly reshaped

America's spiritual landscape, ushering in the era of the First New Age.

Fraternitas Rosae Crucis

Meanwhile, the Fraternitas Rosae Crucis (Fraternity of the Rosy Cross or FRC) stands as the oldest Rosicrucian Order in the United States, founded by Paschal Beverly Randolph in 1856. As a fraternal organization, it operates the Beverly Hall Corporation and the Clymer Health Center in Quakertown, Pennsylvania. The FRC's history traces back to 1861 when its first lodge was established in San Francisco, though it closed shortly after. In 1871, another lodge was founded in Boston, followed by a re-establishment in San Francisco in 1874. Finally, in 1875, the FRC settled in Philadelphia. Under the leadership of Reuben Swinburne Clymer, the FRC found its permanent home at Beverly Hall in Quakertown, Pennsylvania.

'The Fraternitas Rosae Crucis stands as the oldest Rosicrucian Order in the United States, founded by Paschal Beverly Randolph in 1856.'

Throughout its existence, the FRC has been guided by a series of Supreme Grand Masters, each playing a crucial role in shaping the FRC's path and ensuring its enduring continuity over the years. These include:

- Paschal Beverly Randolph (1858–1875)
- Freeman Benjamin Dowd (1875–1907)
- Edward Holmes Brown (1907–1922)
- Reuben Swinburne Clymer (1922–1966)
- Emerson Myron Clymer (1966–1983)
- Gerald Eugene Poesnecker (1983–2003)
- William Glen Kracht (2003–present)

Books by R. Swinburne Clymer:

- *The Thomsonian System of Medicine: With Complete Rules for the Treatment of Disease: Also a Short Materia Medica* (Philosophical Pub. Co., 1905)
- *True Spiritualism* (The Philosophical Publishing Company, 1906)
- *The Philosophy of Fire* (The Philosophical Publishing Co., 1907)
- *Christhood and Adeptship* (The Philosophical Publishing Co., 1910)
- *The Grand Grimore* (The Philosophical Publishing Co., 1910 - under pseudonym "Pythagoras 38")
- *The Rosicrucians, their teachings and mysteries according to the manifestoes issued at various times by the fraternity itself.* Also, some of their secret teachings and the mystery of the order explained... (The Philosophical Pub. Co., 1910)
- *International Esoteric and Illuminated Bible Lessons* (The Philosophical Publishing Co., 1911)
- *The Illuminated Faith: Mystical Interpretation of the Gospel of St. John, in Harmony with Higher Soul Culture and in Accordance with the New Revelation* (Philosophical Publishing Co., 1913)
- *The Way to Life and Immortality; A Positive Philosophy Leading Man Away From "Sin"... and to Manhood, Successful Achievement, Godliness and Immortality* (The Philosophical Publishing Co., 1914)
- *The Way to Godhood: Second Textbook on*

the New Life That Shall Lead Man From Weakness, Disease, and Death, to Freedom From These Things, and to Strength and Power Before Unknown (Allentown, PA: Philosophical Pub. Co., ca. 1914)

- *The Divine Spark, and The Great Pyramid, a Temple of Initiation* (Printed by the Philosophical Publishing Co., 1914)
- *TheÆth Mystery* (The Philosophical Publishing Co., 1914)
- *Making Health Certain; a Philosophical and Inspirational Treatise on the Establishment and Maintenance of Health Through a Constructive Mental Attitude* (The Humanitarian Society, 1921)
- *Mastership, the Divine Law* (Philosophical Pub. Co., 1922)
- *The Book of Rosicruciae; a condensed history of the Fraternitas Rosae Crucis or Rosy Cross, the men who made the order possible, and those who maintained the fraternity throughout the centuries, together with the fundamental teachings of these men according to the actual records in the archives of the fraternity.* Issued by La Fédération universelle des ordres, sociétés et fraternités des initiés. (Philosophical Pub. Co., 1946)
- *The Mystery of Sex and Race Regeneration: A Sane, Sensible and Reasonable Approach to the Highly Important But Much Involved Problem of Sex From The Natural, Moral and Religious Aspects and Having the Regeneration of the Race in View* (fourth edition; Quakertown, PA: Philosophical Pub. Co., 1950)

- *The Mysteries of Osiris; or, Ancient Egyptian Initiation. Setting Forth the Symbolism, Mythology, Legends, and Parables Beginning with the Outer Religious Systems of the Egyptians, Primarily Based on the Drama of the Heavens; Together with the Inner or Esoteric Interpretations as Taught in the Lesser and Greater Mysteries Active Throughout the Ages, Including the Present.* [Completely Rev.] (Philosophical Pub. Co., 1951)
- *The Interpretation of St. John: An Exposition of the Divine Drama; The Nazarene's Life, and What It Teaches to Man* (Philosophical Pub. Co., 1953)
- *Your Health, Your Sanity in the Age of Treason: Food and Liquids Used as a Medium in Deliberately and Carefully Planned Methods Developed by the Vicious Element of Humanity, for the Mental Deterioration and Moral Debasement of the Mass, as a Means Toward Their Enslavement* (Quakertown, PA: Humanitarian Society, c1958)
- *The Age of Treason* (Humanitarian Society, 1959)
- *Nature's Healing Agents: The Medicines of Nature* (or the Natura System) (Philadelphia: Dorrance and Co., c1963)
- *Alchemy and the Alchemists* (AMS Press, 1982)

■

Recommended

Testament of Solomon
A First Century AD Grimoire
Translator: F.C. Conybeare
76 pages, Paperback,
ISBN 9789492355041
www.vamzzz.com

Testament of Solomon could be the oldest of all classical grimoires. The work is one of the so called Pseudepigrapha and should therefore be dated somewhere before the middle of the first century AD, according to the latest research. The book was written in Greek, but most likely the Greek version is a translation of an older version in Hebrew.

Testament of Solomon sums up a list of demonic decan rulers of the Zodiac and provides the method or the invoked angel they can be countered by. This relation between decans and demons or their angelic counterforce is emphasized. Interesting is the relation between the decans and physical complaints. Especially if we compare this text with those of contemporary medical astrology. See Reinhold Ebertin, Enzo Venosta or H.L. Cornell.

The document was translated and first published by F.C. Conybeare in the *Jewish Quaterly Review* of October 1889. Possibly it is the first text that mentions the use of the pentagram (pentalpha) for protection against the evil forces.

VAMzzz Publishing

PAPER BOOKS

VAMzzz Publishing is a publisher that preserves historical occult books and produces new and revised editions in various categories such as Magic & Witchcraft, Secret Rites & Societies, Demonology, Celtic & Mythology, and New Astrology.

Our books are written by highly qualified academic researchers or experts in specific fields of esoteric knowledge, craft, or practice. Many of the revised titles include a Post Scriptum with additional information about the author or subject.

Our reproductions of classic texts differ from others in two important ways. Firstly, we have chosen not to rely on OCR (Optical Character Recognition) technology, as we believe that this often results in poor quality books that are littered with typos and other errors. Secondly, in cases where the original text contains images, such as portraits, maps, or sketches, we have taken great care to preserve the quality of these illustrations, ensuring that they accurately reflect the original artefact. By preserving and sharing these works, we can gain a deeper understanding of our cultural heritage and the rich history of human thought and creativity that has come before us.

In addition to publishing books, VAMzzz Publishing also offers FREE articles on various occult topics, including Afro-American magic, folklore, and New Astrology on our blog. You are welcome to visit vamzzz.com/blog and explore these subjects further.

VAMzzz Publishing
P.O. Box 3340
1001 AC Amsterdam
The Netherlands
vamzzz@protonmail.com
www.vamzzz.com

Incubi and Succubi or Demoniality
A Historical Study of Sexual Contacts with Demons
by Sinistrari of Ameno
194 pages, Paperback, ISBN 9789492355263

This book is a revised English edition of Sinistrari's fascinating 17th century study on the orgasm-stimulating sex demon. The incubus and succubus are the same creature. The intercourse with this astral visitor was called demoniality, a term no longer in use, though nowadays people are still having these mysterious incubus/succubus-"sexperiences".

Mysteria
History of the Secret Doctrines & Mystic Rites of Ancient Religions & Medieval and Modern Secret Orders
by Otto Henne am Rhyn
288 pages, Paperback, ISBN 9789492355225

Mysteria, written in 1869 by Swiss freemason Otto Henne am Rhyn, offers a timeless journey into ancient Egypt, Babylon, and Greek Mystery cults. It explores the Essenes, Orphics, Templars, medieval tribunals, and stone masons. Banned by the Nazis, this historical insider's account remains relevant today.

The Witches of New York
by Q. K. Philander Doesticks P.B.
248 pages, Paperback, ISBN 9789492355348

The Witches of New York portraits a series of psychics, astrologers, and fortunetellers operating within 19th century New York City, written from the perspective of the American humourist Doesticks. The author went from one New York City "witch" (psychic, astrologer, clairvoyant, etc.) to another, to prove how inaccurate they were in their predictions.

www.ingramcontent.com/pod-product-compliance
Ingram Content Group UK Ltd.
Pitfield, Milton Keynes, MK11 3LW, UK
UKHW042008190726
13854UKWH00005B/2212